A TOUR OF THE ARDES

To Nana and Lallie

The WAG numbers after each photograph refer to the Green
Collection held at the Ulster Folk and Transport Museum,
Co. Down, from where prints may be obtained.

This book has received financial assistance under the Cultural
Traditions Programme which aims to encourage acceptance and
understanding of cultural diversity.

Friar's Bush Press
24 College Park Avenue
Belfast BT7 ILR
Published 1990
© Copyright reserved
ISBN 0 946872 30 9

Designed by Rodney Miller Associates, Belfast
Printed by W. & G. Baird, Antrim

Back cover: Strangford Lough at Killyleagh (WAG 2097)
Front cover: The old Market Cross, Newtownards (WAG 945)

A TOUR OF THE ARDES
1910-35

Historic Photographs of the Ards and North-east Down
from the W. A. Green Collection at the
Ulster Folk and Transport Museum.

Jane E. M. Crosbie

FRIAR'S BUSH PRESS

WOMAN AND CHILD EMBROIDERING ON LINEN AT A
COTTAGE IN THE ARDs c.1910 (WAG 294)

A TOUR OF ARDES

'The Ardes of Uladh, scarce and starving, is a country without happiness and without religion.'
This was the pessimistic view of Angus of Satires on the area known as the Ardes in the sixteenth century. The territory then referred to as the Ardes also included what is now known as North Down; however, this part has already been dealt with in my first book of photographs from the W. A. Green collection. The area which is covered in this selection of photographs is from the same collection, and includes the Ards peninsula; the towns of Newtownards and Comber; and finally the coast and islands of north western Strangford Lough leading to the town of Killyleagh. There are some omissions, such as Ardmillan and Ardkeen, but these were made by the photographer not the historian.

William Alfred Green (1870-1958) the photographer, was born into a wealthy middle-class Belfast family. His great uncle was the famous tea-merchant and philanthropist Forster Green; however, William was plagued by ill health as a child and was too sickly for the family business, so he was encouraged to develop his interest in photography into a career. He was trained by R. J. Welch, the leading Ulster photographer, and set up his own commercial studio in 1910. He continued his business until the late 1930s. Many of the photographs featured in this book are of the 'picture postcard' variety and therefore sometimes show an idealised version of life in the Ards in the opening decades of the twentieth century;
aspects of a harsher world, however, do creep in, such as the bare foot children. Green's photographs give a valuable view of the towns, villages and historic ruins of this north eastern region of County Down.

The countryside covered by the photographs is based round the Strangford Lough. In the early Christian period, c.500-1050 A.D., the area was famous for its religious establishments. The monasteries at Nendrum and Movilla, to name just two, were well-respected schools as well as religious establishments and produced such well-known pupils as St Columbanus, St Finian and the great chronicler Marianus Scotus. Their fame also spread, unfortunately, to the Scandanavian countries and the Vikings arrived in the ninth century in search of church treasure. It was the Vikings who gave the lough its present name *Strang-fiord*, or turbulent lough.

The area next attracted special attention to itself in the late twelfth century when both the Plantagenet kings of England and their Anglo-Norman knights (such as the Savage family who settled in the lower half of the peninsula) and O'Neills from county Tyrone became interested in the fertile land and numerous natural harbours. It was around this time that many of the towns and villages featured in the book developed, either around castles (the necessary accessory to conquest, be it from the east or west), harbours or religious establishments, such as Greyabbey and Castleboy.

The next main influx of people came in the early seventeenth century with the official arrival of the Scots. The term official is used here because it would be wrong to expect that the people of the two lands had not intermingled prior to this time, given their close proximity to each other. The official contact, however, arose out of an incident concerning Con O'Neill of Clanaboy [Clandeboye], the then owner of the territory and two Scottish adventurers, James Hamilton and Hugh Montgomery. They agreed to help him escape from Carrickfergus Castle after he had been arrested over an incident with a wine casket and some drunken soldiers. In return for this and also for acting as intermediaries with their 'friend' James I (& VI), Hamilton and Montgomery each received one-third of Con's estate. James Hamilton received what is now known as North Down and Hugh Montgomery obtained most of the area known as the

Ards. They did not, however, win a land flowing with milk and honey, as the territory had been devastated during the wars and rebellions in the mid-sixteenth century, hence Angus's pessimistic view. The pair encouraged the settlement of their land by Scottish farmers and we are informed in the Montgomery manuscripts about *'the substantial persons whom he [Sir Hugh] brought or who came to plant in GreyAbbey, Newtown and corner parishes'* and also that Sir Hugh *'brought with him divers artificers as smiths, masons, carpenters .'*

This influx of Scottish farmers and artisans provides an explanation as to why the predominant religion in the area (with the exception of Portaferry) is Presbyterianism and is also a factor in understanding the support which the United Irishmen's rebellion received in the area, with even Presbyterian ministers participating. Portaferry, however, remained an important area for Roman Catholics in the region. Unlike Con O'Neill the Savage family retained possession of their land, and provided protection for their co-religionists: even after the Savages changed to Protestantism in the late seventeenth century the family continued to be sympathetic landlords to their Roman Catholic tenants.

After the wars of the seventeenth century the area prospered greatly, thanks to the good land, especially suitable for grain crops, which contrasted with the situation elsewhere: we are informed by Alexander Knox that *'as late as the end of the seventeenth century, a great part of the county of Down was still covered with wood, the best cultivated districts being Iveagh, the southern part of Ards and the Lecale.'* The area's economic prosperity was also increased by the growing importance of fabric manufacture, and handloom weavers abounded, working in both linen and imported cotton. This prosperity was reflected in the existence of a customs house at Portaferry.

During the nineteenth century we can note new features of the social and economic life of the Ards. There were important changes in linen production and emigration became significant. Many of the inhabitants had previously found employment as handloom weavers, an occupation which could be carried on in their homes. The growth of weaving factories made life difficult for the independent weavers, a difficulty which was compounded by the great potato famine and the growing trend towards pasture farming which required less labour. This led to growing emigration which continued apace until the 1940s. This emigration took two forms, either migration to large towns within the area, such as Newtownards, Belfast and Killyleagh with their linen mills and factories, or emigration to a different country, be it England, Scotland or further afield. One popular destination for Ards people was Canada. Advertisements appeared, such as this one in the *Newtownards Chronicle* on 2nd April 1910.

ONTARIO: CANADA'S FINEST PROVINCE
WANTED: 500 practical farm labourers immediately, half fare (£4) advanced: 100 domestic servants, full fares advanced.
Situations guaranteed; good wages.

For those who remained there were several avenues of traditional employment such as fishing, farming, distilling or work connected with the linen industry. There were linen mills and factories at Newtownards, Comber and Killyleagh which gave employment to many in their immediate vicinity. However, there was also a flourishing cottage industry for women, namely sprigging or flowering on muslin or linen. Mr & Mrs S. C. Hall, writing in 1846, said that *'Through the whole of this district -the barony of Ards and that of Castlereagh - a large proportion of the peasantry are employed in what is technically termed 'flowering' - embroidering muslin chiefly for the Glasgow manufacturers,*

material and pay fixed sums for the workmanship. The
workers earn generally about 3 shillings a week, a small sum,
but as the majority of the inmates of a cottage are similarly
employed sufficient is obtained to procure the necessities of
life; and indeed some of its luxuries for the interiors of many
of the cabins present all aspects of cheerfulness and
comfort.'

As the linen industry grew so did the demand for what was
known as 'Donaghadee needlework' (so called because it was
originally exported through Donaghadee Harbour). The usual
way of operating was for a company to employ an agent who
lived locally and who would in turn employ local girls and
women. Young girls were taught their skills by older sisters,
mothers and grandmothers.The agent provided the women with
the linen and one resident of Carrowdore remembers, in the
1930's, the women all rushing to see the agent in an attempt to
get 'Initialling' which was better paid than flowering. This
cottage industry was still flourishing in the 1930's. Some of the
material was from Scottish firms but most was from local
mills. The agent was usually employed by a company which
bought the fabric from the mill and then finished it and
distributed the goods. These two advertisements appeared in
the Newtownards Chronicle in 1910.

WANTED: a quantity of special sewers who can sew
monograms and crest-work on handkerchiefs and damask;
highest wages and constant work. Apply John Cully,
Portavogie, or my office Ballywalter.
(The agent was obviously well-known as he did not bother to
include his own name in the advertisement.)

COTTAGE INDUSTRIES: FLOWERING, SPRIGGING
WANTED: Capable agents to give out handkerchiefs for
embroidery: the goods are well paid and provide pleasant
and remunerative occupation for young women in their
homes, liberal commission paid to agents who can get work
done in quantity. Apply McBride & Williams, Ormeau
Avenue, Belfast.

The photographs featured in this selection, taken between 1910
and 1935, reflect a community and way of life which altered
little in the first three decades of the twentieth century.

3

CARROWDORE, MILLISLE, BALLYWALTER AND BALLYHALBERT

Our TOUR OF THE ARDES starts with Carrowdore, Millisle Ballywalter and Ballyhalbert, four villages which reflect the various aspects of life on the peninsula: farming; fishing; and local industry.

During the nineteenth century these villages were all affected by various factors which resulted in a slight decline in population. These included the relocation of the Carmichael flour mill in Millisle to Belfast; better employment prospects in the major towns; and surprisingly, the famine. The general perception is that the eastern counties of Ulster escaped relatively unscathed from the famine: however, the area around Millisle and Carrowdore was badly affected. The reason was that the failure of the potato crop coincided with a period of economic decline, with many hand-loom weavers finding it increasingly difficult to compete with the improvements in technology. The worst hit, however, were better off than many of their compatriots elsewhere, as nowhere on the Ards peninsula was more than 3 miles away from the sea and fishing.

Emigration was not the only source of reduction in population. During the first world war, the villages all lost young men in the trenches and at sea. For example, Shore Street Presbyterian Church, Millisle, lost four men from their congregation with many more wounded, which, when one considers that this was from only one congregation out of a total population of only 255, was clearly devastating. After the war, these coastal villages increasingly found themselves losing their youth to the brighter lights of Belfast and further afield, with the emigration officers being kept busy until well after the second world war.

At the end of the nineteenth century the population of Carrowdore was 502; that of Millisle was 255; Ballywalter 554; and Ballyhalbert 394. Ballywalter and Ballyhalbert were part of the old parish of St Andrews of Inishargy. The tiny church which was built in 1704 is still standing and in use today, although unfortunately W. A. Green did not photograph it. The area also contained the ruins of various ancient ecclesiastical establishments such as Templefinn and Black Abbey (now completely disappeared) which was a Benedictine abbey founded by John de Courcy, Earl of Ulster and husband of Affreca, the foundress of Grey Abbey.

'FLOWERING', CARROWDORE, c.1910 (WAG 1067)
This photograph was taken outside Eliza Margaret Fisher's house in Main Street, Carrowdore. It is unclear whether or not the lady in the photograph is Eliza Fisher. This cottage along with most of the cottages and houses on the left-hand side were knocked down in September 1975 to make way for a housing development. The local linen agent at this time was a Mr Irvine.

THE BARBICAN, CARROWDORE CASTLE (WAG 1855)

CARROWDORE CASTLE c.1920 (WAG 3463)

Carrowdore Castle was built in 1818 for Nicholas de la Cherois Crommelin, a member of the Huguenot family who owned Donaghadee. The family were great benefactors, giving the site of the Presbyterian Church free to the congregation in 1830. The castle passed out of family ownership in the 1930s.

A FARM AND WINDMILL, NEAR MILLISLE c.1910
(WAG 1852)

Millisle developed around windmills, initially, but latterly steam flour mills which were owned by the Messrs Carmichael. The name Millisle, however, would appear to have been derived from a group of rocks just off-shore. The countryside of the Ards is littered with remnants of windmills which were used as a source of power in the absence of running water, up until the late nineteenth century. The prosperity of the farm is reflected in the many outbuildings and slated roofs.

MILLISLE FROM THE SHORE LOOKING SOUTH c.1920
(WAG 3470)

This photograph shows the dual role of the village in the early decades of the twentieth century with the holiday homes on the shore in the foreground and on the far left, in the background, the gable wall of the old Carmichael Mill. W.G. Lyttle said in 1885 that the Millisle was *'quite a favourable resort during summer'*, a popularity which was to develop in the interwar years as public and private transport improved.

SHORE STREET, MILLISLE (WAG 3039)

Shore Street is the oldest residential road in Millisle and many buildings in this photograph date from the late eighteenth and early nineteenth centuries. It is interesting to note the mix of both thatch and slate, industrial and residential buildings. Carmichael's, with the roof off but chimney still standing, is in the centre background. Shore Street Presbyterian Church, whose wall is seen on the right, was first built in 1773. The minister from 1928-57 was the Rev. Thomas Kirkpatrick, an accomplished local historian.

MAIN STREET, MILLISLE (WAG 3040)

This photograph, taken c.1925, shows the main street in Millisle. Although there is no indication of the reason why the crowd has gathered outside John Adam's shop (other than to get their photograph taken) it is possible that they were either holiday makers or day trippers. In 1885 W.G. Lyttle was exhorting his readers to **'not fail to see this quaint little village'** which could be reached by means of the Millisle Car which operated from outside Donaghadee Railway Station.

WOBURN HOUSE AND BEACH, MILLISLE c.1914
(WAG 2087)

Woburn was built in the 1860s for George Dunbar, a former M.P. for Belfast. When this photograph was taken the house was owned by George's daughter and son-in-law, Georgina and Charles Dunbar-Buller. The house was later owned by the Pack Beresford family who sold it in 1956 to the Ministry of Finance and it became a borstal for a time.

THE STRAND, BALLYWALTER (WAG 1866)

This view of the town, taken on the road from Millisle, has remained largely unaltered over the years. The town, in common with many on the eastern coast of the Ards peninsula, developed in a strip along the coastline. The town is described in Shaw's tourist guide of c.1877 as having *'One well-laid out street, the houses nearly all on the same side, fronting the sea'*. The Holy Trinity Church of Ireland church, seen on the right, was erected in 1826.

BALLYWALTER FROM THE SHORE (WAG 1747)

In 1885 W.G. Lyttle lamented the fact that so few people were able to reach the town. However, by the interwar years and the 1940s, with improvements in public and private transport Ballywalter became increasingly popular as a holiday destination.

BALLYWALTER MAIN STREET (WAG 1748)
This photograph taken c.1910 shows the main street with a mix of two-storey houses and thatched cottages. In the mid-nineteenth century Ballywalter was quite a thriving port. The harbour was built in 1851 and Lewis in 1846 records that the town had a *'coast guard station, forming one of the twelve that constitute the District of Donaghadee.'*

BALLYWALTER MAIN STREET LOOKING NORTH
(WAG 1749)

This photograph, taken c.1925, shows the Presbyterian Church on the left. Ballywalter was one of Ireland's oldest congregations, having been formed in 1626. This church building was erected in 1889 for the second Ballywalter congregation which had split from the original in 1820 and reunited a century later on 15 May 1925. The spire was provided by the widow of a former minister, Mrs Henry Gamble, who was also a generous benefactress of the Presbyterian College in Belfast.

DUNLEATH ARMS HOTEL (WAG 1750)

This hotel, built in 1902, was one of only two licensed premises in the area. R.L. Praegar in 1900 said: *'the neat little town of Ballywalter [is] locally celebrated as possessing no policeman, no doctor and only two licensed houses'*. The Dunleath Arms belonged to the Ulster Public Houses Trust Co. Ltd., which followed the so-called ***Pro Bono Publico*** school of temperance reformers, and advertised widely that ***'Tea, Coffee, Bovril, &c., always ready, and sold as cheaply and as willingly as alcoholic drink.' 'No push, no adulteration, no tick'. 'Surplus profits to be eventually spent on objects of public utility or charity'.***

WELL ROAD, BALLYWALTER (WAG 1779)

This photograph of Ballywalter is different from the others because it was obviously not taken for commercial purposes. There is a nice contrast between the sturdy but small houses in the foreground and the large villas in the middle. Well Road led down to the shore and the occupants of the villas would have had a good view of the yachting regattas which started c.1880 and were held annually.

BALLYWALTER PARK (WAG 1876)

Originally called Springvale, this house was erected in 1805 and considerably altered by Sir Charles Lanyon, the famous architect, in 1848. The house and estate were bought on 6 April 1846 for £23,00 by Andrew Mulholland, who not only improved the house but also laid out the parkland, planting 93,500 trees and shrubs. Andrew Mulholland was a founder of the York Street Flax Spinning Co. Ltd. His son, John, was created Baron Dunleath of Ballywalter in 1892.

BALLYHALBERT, CO. DOWN (WAG 1871)
This photograph was taken c.1910. The little girl at the pump
is Lizzie Millar who lived in the town but later emigrated.

20

BALLYHALBERT, 1935 (WAG 2725)

The village was still primarily a fishing village but by 1935 it was also being increasingly viewed as a holiday destination with its long sandy beaches and relatively safe bathing providing the attraction. The first electricity cable to a house in the village was not laid until February 1949. Mains water also did not arrive in the village until after the second world war.

PORTAVOGIE, KIRKISTOWN, CASTLEBOY, CLOGHY AND QUINTIN

As we move down the eastern coast of the Ards Peninsula we reach Portavogie, Kirkistown, Castleboy, Cloghy and Quintin. These contain a mixture of the the remains of defensive Anglo-Norman castles and ecclesiastical establishments, and modern fishing villages.

This area of Ulster was settled by the Anglo-Normans in the twelfth century but they came increasingly under attack from the O'Neills, originally from Tyrone, who were also colonising the region. The Savages, who held the Peninsula, built a series of defensive forts or castles, of which Kirkistown and Quintin alone in this area remain. Both were altered in the nineteenth century, although Kirkistown retains much of its original shape.

The harbour at Portavogie is well-known; however, less famous is the fact that the harbour at Cloghy was also used by the local farmers to export their produce and import commodities such as coal. The state of the roads in the peninsula was poor until the end of the nineteenth century which meant that it was easier and cheaper to send one's goods by sea than by road. As methods of communication improved the sea trade declined although local fishing boats still used the facilities.

The area was one of ecclesiastical importance in ancient and medieval times. The old church at Castleboy was the only Preceptory of the Knights of St. John of Jerusalem in the entire diocese of Down and Connor.

During the period 1910 to 1930 the area did not really alter; however, it did become more popular as a destination for holidays and day trips. Richard Hayward in his book **In Praise of Ulster (1938)** mentions the area thus **'Cloghy (the place of stones) where there is a nice sandy eighteen-hole golf course. Close to this golf course is the ruin of Kirkistown Castle. built by Roland Savage in 1622 . . .'**

The photographs of the area taken by W. A. Green reflect all aspects of life, from the romantic architecture of Quintin Castle to the fishing fleet of Portavogie at low tide.

KIRKISTOWN CASTLE (WAG 3144)

Kirkistown castle was built by Roland Savage in the early 1600s and was described by the author of the Montgomery Manuscripts as a *'high square pile.'* Harris writing in 1744 records *'within the circuit of it a good Dwelling House of* *Mrs Lucy Magil, now the Widow Savage.'* The dwelling house may be seen on the right with the horse and cart outside. At the beginning of the nineteenth century the tower was altered in the Gothic Revival style.

PORTAVOGIE HARBOUR (WAG 2659)

Portavogie grew up around a natural harbour which was protected by 20 feet high rocks. The majority of the inhabitants were employed by fishing and in 1886 G.H. Bassett recorded that *'about 40 fishing luggers hail from here. They go to Kinsale in Spring and to the Shetland Islands in Summer.'*

HERRING BOATS IN PORTAVOGIE HARBOUR
(WAG 3073)

Another view of the harbour. The man-made harbour at Portavogie was not built until c.1900 and the fleet dates only from the mid-nineteenth century. A point to note is the fishing nets drying on the harbour wall.

CASTLEBOY (WAG 1869)

This ruin was owned in 1910 by the Echlin family but was originally the castle and church of the Ardes Preceptory of the Knights of St John of Jerusalem, The order was established here in the latter half of the twelfth century by Hugh de Lacy, an Anglo-Norman, and later Earl of Ulster. The buildings fell into ruins after the dissolution of the monasteries in the sixteenth century.

CLOGHY BAY, CO. DOWN (WAG 3036)
The village developed along the curve of a beautiful sandy beach, unfortunately not shown here. In 1881 the population was 150. The church building on the right is the Presbyterian Church whose congregation was not formed until 1841.

CLOGHY BAY (WAG 1851)

c.1910 Cloghy was a small fishing village with nine fishing luggers and 30 row-boat fishermen, but in the nineteenth century the natural harbour was also used for discharging coal and the local farmers were able to export their produce. This delightful photograph shows both aspects of this life with fishermen's cottages set against a background of farmland.

QUINTIN BAY CASTLE (WAG 3256)

Quintin Castle was one of a group of defensive castles built in the early 1600s by Roland Savage and occupied by the Smiths. It was sold to the Montgomerys in the seventeenth century. It later fell into disrepair until it was completely renovated in the 1870s by a Mr Calvert, in this wonderfully romantic version of a castle - the original having been a simple tower house. The castle was owned in the 1920s by the King Hall family whose daughter Magdalene achieved early fame as the author of an historical account of early eighteenth century Co, Down life, which turned out to be fictitious. Her later novel *The life and death of the wicked Lady Skelton* (1944) was very successful and was made into a film starring the late Margaret Lockwood.

PORTAFERRY

Portaferry lies at the mouth of Strangford Lough and its castle, together with that of Strangford, has stood guard over the lough and its environs for centuries.

Portaferry developed around a castle built in the twelfth century by the Savages, an Anglo-Norman family. The Savage/Nugent family have had a major influence over the town up to the last quarter of the twentieth century. Most of the present town dates from the eighteenth and nineteenth centuries when the town was a thriving port complete with its own customs house. This had not always been the case, as the writer of the Montgomery Manuscripts explains: *'Patrick's [Savage] estate was much in debt, and not one stone walled house in that town, only some fishermen's cabins and an old Irish castle out of repair near it, nor any mills and very little grain to employ one .. and no trade by sea (nor encouragement for it) before the said year 1623.'* Patrick Savage's brother-in-law, Sir James Montgomery, set about putting things to right.

The prosperity which resulted from the efforts of Sir James and later the Savage family continued until the advent of steam-powered shipping which needed deeper harbours, although Portaferry's importance as a link between the peninsula and south Down continued. Just as Portaferry's importance as a port and trading centre faded, so her population declined from a peak of 2,203 in 1831 to only 1,518 in 1911.

The Portaferry which W. A. Green has captured is not very much different to the one with which we are familiar, although nowadays the boats are not quite so imposing. Yet again there are some omissions in the collection; for example, the Market House, which dates form the mid-eighteenth century and which housed a garrison of troops who successfully repelled an attack by the United Irishmen in 1798. Also omitted are the famous Whale Bones at Ballywhite Bay, which formed an arch and were a popular attraction.

The photographs which W. A. Green did take, however, truly reflect what Bassett described as *'among the most charmingly picturesque places in Ireland.'*

PORTAFERRY CASTLE (WAG 601)

Portaferry Castle was built in the sixteenth century by Patrick Savage, Lord Savage of the little Ardes, who died in 1603. It was renovated by Sir James Montgomery who was brother-in-law to the then owner, also called Patrick, in 1635. It was still used as a residence in 1744 when Walter Harris reported that it *'is now inhabitated by Andrew Savage Esq.'* and Arthur Young stayed there on 28 July 1776 while on his tour of Ireland.

PORTAFERRY CASTLE FROM THE QUAY (WAG 602)

An interesting view of the castle and part of both Castle Street and Strand Street from the quay. The schooner, *The Mayflower*, is tied up at the quay. The house on the left is called Whaparilla and was built in the mid-nineteenth century. It is now part of The Queen's University Marine Biology Station.

BALLYPHILLIP CHURCH OF IRELAND CHURCH, PORTAFERRY (WAG 603)

The authors of the Ulster Architectural Heritage Society's survey of Portferry and Strangford have described this church as *'a very good example of the simple unassuming Irish Parish churches of the late Georgian period.'* It was built in 1787 at a cost of the £883 18s 9d to replace the existing church at Templecraney which was in bad repair. Initially it had a spire but this was removed c.1810 and the chancel and transept were added in the 1870s. The church is dedicated to St James, and it contains many memorials to members of the Nugent/Savage family, including the last two of the male line who were killed in action within 18 months of each other in 1943-4.

ROMAN CATHOLIC CHURCH, PORTAFERRY (WAG 604)

Writing in 1744 Walter Harris said that there was a *'Mass-house near the town and (which is singular) it is the only place in the Ardes where there is any mass-house.'* This church is reputed to stand on the same site and the datestone is inscribed 'A.D. 1762', although it has been much altered since then. The bell-tower, sacristy, chancel and side-chapels were all added in 1914 which puts this photograph at c.1918, owing to the newish appearance of the stonework.

TEMPLECRANEY CHURCH, PORTAFERRY (WAG 605)

Templecraney was originally a medieval church and later served as the Church of Ireland parish church until the erection of St James' church in 1787. The ruins are on the left side of Church Street and R. L. Praegar in 1900 remarked that *'one high ivy-clad fragment of a gable wall still stands surmounted by a small bell-cote.'* The gravestones belong to both Protestants and Roman Catholics.

PORTAFERRY FROM BEACH (WAG 608)
An attractive view of the town from the beach. Most of the buildings at this end of the street are private residences, predominantly two or three storeyed, slate-roofed and mid-Victorian. The castle tower is visible in the distance.

SHORE STREET, PORTAFERRY, LOOKING NORTH
(WAG 609)

Taken from the start of Shore Street this view shows the slipway as well a the larger pier. Portaferry had flourished in the eighteenth and early nineteenth century largely as a result of the plans of Sir James Montgomery in the 1620s and 1630s, who put the town on a business footing (after his brother-in-law, Patrick Savage, had become almost bankrupt and had been sent to live on the Isle of Man), and also the good efforts of later generations of the Savage family.

SHORE STREET FROM THE QUAY (WAG 611)
A view from the quay. On the left hand side is one of the two eighteenth century houses which became the Portaferry Hotel. The tower of St Patrick's Roman Catholic Hall, which was built in 1900 is visible on the right.

PORTAFERRY HARBOUR (WAG 612)

Portaferry's harbour had its heyday in the eighteenth and nineteenth centuries, but trade waned with the advent of steam shipping. There was a Customs House in Portaferry in 1744 and as late as the 1880s there were eight luggers and twenty rowboats. The Nugents owned both the harbour and the pier.

THE NUGENT ARMS AND MOTOR BUS (WAG 613)
This photograph must have taken some time between 1908 and
1916 as it was during these years that J.B. Ferguson and Hugh
Graham operated their Reliance buses between Newtownards
and Portaferry.

NUGENT ARMS, PORTAFERRY (WAG 614)
A similar view but taken in the 1930s, as can be seen by the
Ards Motor Co. bus which started its service in 1917 and also

the Belfast Bank, the red-brick building on the right, which
was built in 1930.

PORTAFERRY HOUSE (WAG 2714)

This house was built in 1821 by William Farrell for the Nugent family. The Savages changed their name from Savage to Nugent in 1797 and presumably their behaviour, as may be surmised by the saying prevalent at the time: *'I'd rather have an old Savage than a new gent.'* The house has only recently been sold by the Nugent family.

PORTAFERRY FROM STRANGFORD (WAG 2748)

This picturesque view of Portaferry shows the extent of the town. The tower on the hill is a disused windmill which was originally built in 1771 and abandoned in 1838. There has been a ferry service between Portaferry and Strangford for several centuries. Walter Harris in 1744 recorded that *'a ferry-boat maintains a constant communication between the Baronies of Lecale and Ardes.'*

KIRCUBBIN, GREYABBEY, MOUNTSTEWART, LOUGHRIES AND MOVILLA

These five places of interest all lie on the western side of the Ards peninsula.

The town of Kircubbin is perhaps the odd one out in this group as Samuel Lewis's *Topographical dictionary of Ireland* of 1846 explains: *'This town is of very recent origin, having been built since the year 1790, previously to which time there were not more than five houses in the place. The present town contains 136 houses for the greater part neatly built.'* Kircubbin became a thriving market town and harbour: a special export in the mid-nineteenth century was kelp of which great quantities were burned and sent to Liverpool.

By contrast the two abbeys of Movilla and Greyabbey are centuries old. The former dates from the sixth century and the latter from the twelfth.

The area is also famous for some of its past inhabitants who were involved in events of national and international importance. It was a centre for activity by the United Irishmen, and Robert Stewart, Lord Castlereagh, who played such an important role in the history of both Britain and Ireland, was reared in Mountstewart.

Mountstewart, the seat of the Londonderry family, is situated half way between Greyabbey and Movilla. It was during the 1920s, when most of these photographs were taken, that the famous gardens were laid out to the designs of Edith, Lady Londonderry. In Greyabbey is Rosemount, the seat of the Montgomery family, who played such a vital role in the history of the entire area. Writing in 1701 William Montgomery in his Description of the Barony called the Ardes tells that *'King James, granted a port to be at GreyAbbey Islands with pilotage, anchorage, keelage and other advantages and privileges to the same and licensed exportation of all native commodities thereout (except Irish yarn) but there is no trade there at this time. The market day of GreyAbbey is on Friday but as little regarded as the port.'* By 1886 Bassett was reporting that Greyabbey was *'one of the handsomest villages in the County,'* a statement reflected in the photographs taken by W. A. Green.

Most of the photographs shown in this chapter could have been taken recently as, fortunately, this area has changed so little in appearance in the last seventy years.

KIRCUBBIN (WAG 1834)

Kircubbin developed rapidly in the early nineteenth century, centred around the harbour and local industries such as linen. Lewis reported in 1846 that *'the inhabitants carry on a small but prosperous trade. The manufacture of straw hats and bonnets . . . affords employment to most of the industrious female population of the town and adjoining parishes.'* By the late nineteenth century this alternative source of employment had largely stopped.

MAIN STREET, KIRCUBBIN (WAG 1835)

This photograph was taken at the top of the Main Street, a pleasant road with two-storey buildings which were built in the early nineteenth century. The 'Rosemount' cycle shop betrays the Montgomerys' influence in the peninsula despite the fact that the town was actually owned by this stage by the Ward family from Bangor.

MAIN STREET, KIRCUBBIN (WAG 1837)
Another view of the Main Street, this time looking north. The house in the centre is the Presbyterian manse which was built c.1850. Lewis recorded in 1846 **'A market-house with a** **brown linen hall in the rear of it'** which was supposed to have been near this site, but no trace of it remains.

STRANGFORD LOUGH FROM KIRCUBBIN (WAG 1836)
A delightful composition no doubt for use as a postcard. Points
to note include the pony and trap and the boats moored on the
islands.

KIRCUBBIN HARBOUR (WAG 1838)

Kircubbin harbour was owned by the Ward family of Bangor Castle. In the 1880s, Bassett recorded the import of coal, salt and Indian corn and the export of grains, beans and potatoes from the harbour. In addition there were numerous fishing boats registered here. Trade continued at the harbour until the 1930s.

GREYABBEY (WAG 3038)

W.G. Lyttle described Greyabbey as *'a romantic little village.'* In the eighteenth century, life in the village was based on a flourishing fabric trade. Lewis recorded in 1846 that *'a great quantity of calico and muslin is woven by the peasantry at their own dwellings.'* The Presbyterian church building is on the right. A former minister, James Porter, was a famous pamphleteer and was executed for his involvement in the United Irishmen's rebellion of 1798.

GREYABBEY (WAG 329)

The Cistercian monastery at Greyabbey was founded in 1193 by Affreca, who was the daughter of the King of Man and wife of John de Courcy, Earl of Ulster. The monastery flourished until it was dissolved in 1541. The buildings, in common with many in the area, were burnt in 1572 by Sir Brian Mac Phelim O'Neill to prevent them being used as a refuge by English troops.

GREYABBEY FROM THE SOUTH (WAG 332A)

The Montgomeries built a mansion house beside the ruins of Greyabbey in 1634; however, this was burnt down and the present house of Rosemount was not built until 1762. The family restored part of the ruins of the abbey for use as a parish church until 1778 and most of the family are buried inside the ruined church.

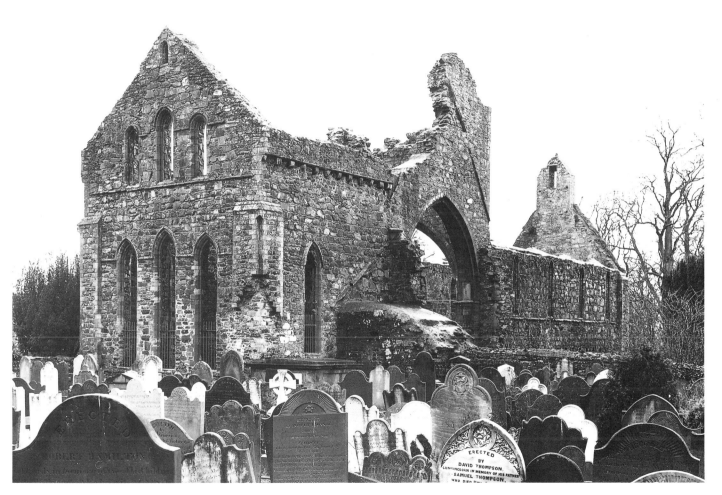

GREYABBEY (WAG 333)

This view was taken from in front of the present Church of Ireland church, which was built in 1778. The churchyard continued in use to the opening decades of the twentieth century.

DOLMEN, MOUNTSTEWART (WAG 44)

This dolmen is all that is left of a prehistoric cemetery which was found in the grounds of Mountstewart in 1786. It was in the centre and its chamber was at least twice as large as the others, presumably denoting someone of importance. The others were dismantled as the stones were needed to fill a drain.

TEMPLE OF THE WINDS, MOUNTSTEWART (WAG 949)

'On the summit of an eminence in the grounds is an elegant building, a model of the Temple of the Winds at Athens, erected under the personal superintendence of J. Stewart Esq., whose skill and taste in Grecian architecture procured for him the appelation of the Athenian Stewart; it is built of stone from the quarries of Scrabo and the floors, which are *of bog fir found in the peat-moss on the estate, are, for beauty of material and elegance of design, unequalled by anything of the kind in the country.'* Samuel Lewis, *Topographical dictionary of Ireland,* (1846, revised edition, London).

MOUNTSTEWART (WAG 948)

Here we see the main facade of Mountstewart which was the seat of the Londonderry family. The original parts of the house date from the years 1803-06 with the rest of the house dating from 1825-8, when the 3rd Marquis, who was Lord Castlereagh's half-brother, decided to enlarge the property. The interior was redecorated in the 1920s by Edith, Lady Londonderry, who came to live at Mountstewart in 1921. The house was given to the National Trust in 1977.

MOUNTSTEWART (WAG 948)

This photograph shows part of the famous gardens which were laid out, starting c.1921, by Edith, Lady Londonderry, whose husband, Charles, was Minister for Education in the Northern Ireland government and British Air Minister in the 1930s. The gardens were given to the National Trust of Northern Ireland in 1957.

LINEN EMBROIDERING, LOUGHRIES (WAG 292)

The family featured in this photograph are the McKeags. The old man was James McKeag, a retired professional soldier, and his wife, Jane, is standing beside him. Two of their daughters, Bella and Martha, are also featured in the photograph. The present owner of the cottage is the grandson of James and Jane and has dated the photograph at c.1914, as his grandfather died c.1915. The building in the background is Loughries National School, now the Primary School.

EMBROIDERING A BEDSPREAD, LOUGHRIES
(WAG 293)

The family featured in this photograph were the Kilpatricks. The man and woman were Willy and Mary and the two children seen here were Jean and Leslie. The family lived in this house on the Ballyhaft Road in Loughries until 1931 when the house was sold.

MOVILLA ABBEY (WAG 943)

Movilla Abbey was reputedly founded by St Finian in 550 A.D. and became one of the greatest schools in Ireland. Two of its more famous pupils were St Columbanus (who is reputed to have turned water into wine while resident here) and Marianus Scotus whose chronicle (written 1052-83) is one of the greatest historical accounts of medieval times.

ANGLO-NORMAN GRAVE SLAB-FEMALE, MOVILLA
(WAG 24)
This grave slab probably belonged to an Anglo-Norman lady,
but definitely belonged to a female as may be ascertained by
the presence of shears. It was imbedded in the walls of the
ruins along with several others, in the 1880s, to preserve it.

NEWTOWNARDS, SCRABO AND COMBER

Newtownards and Comber both lie at the northern end of Strangford Lough with the vantage point of Scrabo hill between them. Both towns have played important roles in the development of the area.

The 'New town' of Ards was established in the twelfth century when a village grew up around a castle which was erected by the Anglo-Norman settlers. The Anglo-Normans, under Walter de Burgh, also endowed a Dominican Priory in 1244 which, according to Rev. James O'Laverty, *'became celebrated among the Dominicans. In it were held Great Chapters in 1298 and 1312.'* The priory was dissolved during the reign of Henry VIII and, along with many more in the area, it was burnt in 1572. The Montgomery family obtained Newtownards in the seventeenth century but the author of the Montgomery Manuscript said that *'30 cabins could not be found. nor any stone walls. but ruined roofless churches . . and a stump of an old castle in Newtown, in each of which some Gentlemen sheltered themselves at their first coming over.'*

Similarly Comber also developed around an ecclesiastical establishment; however, in this case it was somewhat more ancient, having reputedly been founded by St Patrick. The Montgomery family also owned Comber and in 1675 they sold both Comber and Newtownards to Sir Robert Colville and eventually the towns were bought by the Stewarts (later the Londonderry's) in the 1740s. The Montgomeries retained, however, ownership of the Mount Alexander estate until it too passed out of family hands, this time through marriage and inheritance to the Delacherois Crommelin family, owners of Donaghadee and Carrowdore. The mansion house of Mount Alexander, which was originally erected using stones from the ruins of the abbey, had itself become ruinous by the mid-nineteenth century and no trace now exists.

The nineteenth century was a period of growth for both towns, with the population of Newtownards growing from 4,442 in 1831 to 7,621 in 1841 and levelling out at about 9,000 at the turn of the century. By 1926 the population of Newtownards was 10,149. The population in Comber grew from 1,713 in 1861 to 2,006 in 1871 and by 1926 it was 2,684. The rapid expansion may be attributed to a number of factors such as the development of local industries like distilling and linen and, importantly, the arrival of the railway, in 1850 at Newtownards and in 1861 at Comber.

Newtownards, especially, was very prosperous and was the third largest town in Co. Down in the nineteenth century, the other two being Newry and Downpatrick. It was the main market town in the area for farm produce as well as being a centre for all aspects of linen production. The newspapers from 1910-1930 repeatly carry reports about flax production, adverts for linen and muslin agents and of course factories such as that of the Ards Weaving Company. Comber was also important as a centre for linen production with the large Andrews flax spinning mill established there. The mill's close proximity to the railway station ensured rapid delivery of goods. The quarries at Scrabo provided employment to many in the area and Scrabo stone was a ready source of building material, as may be seen by the buildings in the Ards area.

The photographs which W. A. Green took of Newtownards, Scrabo and Comber reflect very accurately many aspects of life in the area, from the Scrabo Golf Links to the market days.

NEWTOWNARDS PRIORY (WAG 1792)

The Newtownards Priory was founded in 1244 by Walter de Burgh, Earl of Ulster, but after its dissolution in 1541, the priory was burnt in 1572. The Montgomeries acquired the town and, according to the *Montgomery Manuscripts,*

'In Summer 1608, some of the priory walls were roofed and fitted for his [Sir Hugh's] lady and children and servants (which were many) to live in.' This house was burnt in 1644.

CHANCEL, NEWTOWNARDS PRIORY (WAG 50)

This aisle was added in the thirteenth century by the Dominicans who owned the priory, and the arches are fine examples of Anglo-Norman architecture. Services were held in the priory until 1817 and the site was used as a private burial site after 1860 by the Londonderry family.

OLD PRIORY, NEWTOWNARDS (WAG 944)
This view of the Priory was taken from Court Street. The old
Priory was used as a court house from 1817 to 1850. The tower
was added to the original structures by Sir Hugh Montgomery

in the seventeenth century. The Georgian houses on the right
are still standing but are in a rather dilapidated looking state.

OLD MARKET CROSS, NEWTOWNARDS c.1910
(WAG 945)

The old Market Cross stands at the junction of Movilla Street, High Street and Church Street. It is a hexagonal structure and the coat of arms of the Montgomery family may be seen here. This market cross was built in 1666 by the residents on the exact site of the original cross which had been destroyed. The inscription on one of its sides read *Theis Arms, which rebels* *threw down and defac'd 1653 Are by this Loyal Burrowgh now replac'd - 1666 W. B. Proweft-Deus nobis haec otia fecit.* Note the barefooted children: in 1910 there were about 550 people on outdoor relief in the town and surrounding poor law union area.

THE MARKET HOUSE FROM THE SQUARE,
NEWTOWNARDS (WAG 946)

The original Market House was beside the market cross. However, this was replaced in 1771 by the existing Market House/Town Hall which was designed by Ferdinando Stratford in 1765; the cupola was added in 1778. It has been described by Sir Charles Brett in his study of Ulster Court and Market Houses as the finest market house in the province. The weekly market is held in the square every Saturday.

SCRABO HILL WITH LONDONDERRY MONUMENT.
(WAG 947)

A scenic view taken on the road out of Newtownards which shows the extent to which the Londonderry Monument dominated the skyline in the surrounding area, so much that it was used as a navigational aid in both peace and war times.

LONDONDERRY MONUMENT, SCRABO (WAG 1785)
The Londonderry monument was built in 1859 to designs by
Charles Lanyon, in memory of General Charles William Vane-
Stewart, the 3rd and so-called 'Fighting' Marquis of
Londonderry who had not only distinguished himself in the
Peninsula Wars but had also fought a duel with Henry Grattan.
The view from the top of Scrabo is spectacular and on a clear
day it is possible to see both Scotland and the Isle of Man.
Until quite recently cream teas were served in the tower.

SCRABO GOLF LINKS (WAG 1786)

The Scrabo Golf Club was founded on 13 December 1907 and was the brainchild (or storm, given the location) of Hugh Simms and Gerald S. Netterfield, both natives of Newtownards. Famous past members include Blair Mayne the second world war hero. Richard Hayward in *In Praise of Ulster* (1938) states: *'all year round the tower is a splendid nine-hole golf course with greens that are a delight to play but with some narrow, rock-bound fairways that will drive you mad unless you hit a straight ball. This is a marvellous spot to play a quiet nine-holes, have a nice little country meal in the tower, play another nine-holes and all the while drink in the glorious sweep of landscape which is with you on every hand. '*

70

HARVEST NEAR SCRABO (WAG 3292)

The land around Newtownards and Comber is amongst the
most fertile in County Down. As well as the usual arable crops,
seen here, the land was extensively used for the growing of
flax to supply the ever increasing demands made by the linen
mills in Belfast and closer to home. In addition, hundreds of
acres were used as bleaching greens and were directly owned
by the larger mills.

COMBER RIVER (WAG 2741)

The name Comber is actually derived from **comar,** meaning a confluence of two rivers which then became the Esler or Comber River. The river was instrumental in the economic prosperity of the town in the nineteenth century as small boats brought coal in and oats and potatoes out. This died out at the turn of the century with the improvement of road and rail links.

THE GILLESPIE MONUMENT, COMBER (WAG 1781)
The monument to Major-General Robert Rollo Gillespie which stands in the middle of the town square was erected in 1845 in memory of Comber's most famous and colourful local character. Rollo Gillespie was a hero in the romantic, swashbuckling mould. He had a wide military career, including, fighting duels, eloping, fighting pirates in the Carribean, and, finally, falling fatally wounded while commanding the Meerut division of the Benegal troops in the war against Nepal, gasping with his dying breath, *'One shot more for the honour of Down.'*

THE SQUARE, COMBER (WAG 876)

This view of the square shows the Gillespie Monument with the Church of Ireland church in the background on the left. The church was built on the site of a twelfth century Cistercian Abbey which was endowed by the White family in 1198. After the dissolution the abbey was destroyed but part of the ruins were used by Sir Hugh Montgomery to build a parish church; the rest of the ruins were used in the building of his mansion Mount Alexander which has now completely disappeared.

74

MAIN STREET, COMBER (WAG 877)

Despite being described by Walter Harris as a *'mean little village'* with *'no trade'* in 1744, by the mid-nineteenth century Comber had become a thriving market town and in 1886 amongst its other assets G.H. Bassett listed *'extensive spinning mills, whisky distilleries and agencies for sewed muslin and a mineral water factory.'* The good behaviour of the residents was apparent from a headline in the *Newtownards Chronicle* on 28 February 1920: *'Comber Petty Sessions - Good Record sustained - More Justices Cases!'*

CASTLE ESPIE, NENDRUM, SKETRICK, RINGHADDY AND KILLYLEAGH

The north-western shoreline of Strangford Lough is littered with reminders of civilisations long gone and almost forgotten. The fertile land and safe anchorage on Strangford, provided a focus for early settlers who farmed and traded here. Reminders of the area's history are scattered along the shore in the shape of dolmens and ruined churches.

The area, in modern historical times, was originally settled by the Anglo-Normans, led by John de Courcy, Earl of Ulster, who, with his followers, erected a chain of defensive forts and castles along the coast. Traces of these still remain but perhaps the best known castle is the marvelously fairy-talesque Killyleagh Castle. It was originally built by the Mandevilles, an Anglo-Norman family, but changed hands and shape several times until it eventually came into the possession of the Hamilton family in 1610. They have retained possession ever since apart from briefly losing control of it to the Cromwellians in 1649.

Killyleagh, which R. L. Praegar described as *'a busy little town'* had a population of 1,513 at the end of the nineteenth century and a thriving linen industry both in the town itself and also in nearby Shrigley, which had been purpose built by Mr Martin to serve his mill. According to Samuel Lewis in 1846 there were *'13,798 spindles employing 186 persons and 244 power looms attended by 156 persons constantly engaged in weaving printers cloths for the Manchester market; and connected with this manufactory are more than 2,000 handlooms in the neighbouring-districts.'* In 1886 G. H. Bassett recorded that some 150 people were employed by

sewed muslin agents. The town also had a busy harbour which dealt mainly with imports such as coal and salt.

Killyleagh was also the birthplace of several famous people, in particular Sir Hans Sloane (born 1666), a founder of the British Museum and the man after whom Sloane Square in London is named.

The photographs which W. A. Green took of this area are mainly picturesque views destined for postcards; however, there are a couple which are very unusual.

THE FIVE SISTERS STONE CIRCLE, NEAR COMBER
(WAG 881)
Samuel Lewis in 1846 recorded that **'Numerous forts and raths are scattered over the parish. There is a large Druidical alter at Ballygraphen, the table-stone of which,** now lying on the ground, measures 19 feet by 6 and is 4 feet thick: the five upright stones are in an adjoining hedge row'. The stones are known as the five sisters.

STANDING STONE, CASTLE ESPIE (WAG 43)

Castle Espie is a site of great geological importance as it is one of only three outcrops of Carboniferous rocks in County Down. The limestone was extensively worked throughout the centuries but by 1900 the quarries were lying idle and Castle Espie began to attract visitors because of the natural beauty of the area. Nowadays, the visitors are attracted by the bird sanctuary and the conservation area.

RINGNEAL BRIDGE, NEAR COMBER (WAG 878)
Leaving Castle Espie the road meanders through the rolling drumlins and innumerable islands of the Strangford shore, towards the ancient ecclesiastical settlement of Nendrum on Mahee Island.

BELFAST NATURALIST FIELD CLUB AT MAHEE
9 SEPTEMBER 1922 (WAG 3049)

This photograph was dated July by the photographer but this is incorrect as may be seen from the following extract from the B.N.F.C. proceedings for the year 1922: *'Nendrum - the club joined with the Archaeological Section of the Belfast Natural History and Philosophical Society in a excursion to Nendrum, Mahee Island on 9th September 1922. Rev. Canon Carmody and Mr H.C. Lawlor gave addresses explanatory of the history of this ancient monastic foundation and described the results of the excavations recently made.'*

CHURCH AND ROUND TOWER, MAHEE ISLAND
(WAG 3525)

The monastic settlement of Nendrum on Mahee Island is thought to have been founded c450 A.D. by St. Mochaoi who had been converted by St. Patrick. As with many other monastic settlements in Ireland it became a great centre of learning with, amongst others, St. Finnian of Movilla as a past pupil. According to the *Historic Monuments of Northern Ireland*, it remains the best example in Northern Island of a pre-Norman monastic enclosure with its buildings.

MAHEE CASTLE (WAG 2091)
Mahee Castle was built in 1570 by an English soldier, Captain
Browne. It stands guard over the causeway to Island Reagh.

SKETRICK ISLAND, STRANGFORD LOUGH (WAG 2724)

R. L. Praegar described Sketrick Castle as *'one of the strongest of the 27 fortresses that the Anglo-Normans built on Strangford lough after John de Courcy's invasion.'* Part of the south-western side of the castle fell down in 1896 and it was feared that the rest would follow but it has withstood the urge for destruction.

RINGHADDY CASTLE, KILLINCHY (WAG 2001)
Ringhaddy castle was another defensive fort although it would appear to have been occupied longer than the others. The farmhouse on the left was built in the 1880s or 1890s as Praegar referred to it as modern in 1900. Ringhaddy used to be famous for its native oysters.

RINGHADDY OLD CHURCH (WAG 2002)

The ruins of this church date from Anglo-Norman times; no doubt it was built for the use of the occupants of the castle.

Rev. James O'Laverty reported that in the taxation of Pope Nicholas **'the church of Rencady'** was valued at 40s.

KILLYLEAGH CASTLE (WAG 1697)

This photograph of Killyleagh Castle was taken from the south. The castle in its present form was built 1847-51 to designs by Charles Lanyon; however, a castle in some form ranging from a round tower to a *'Mere mansion battlemented along the summit'* has stood on this site since the twelfth century. Originally built by the Mandevilles, ownership of the castle passed to the Whytes and finally in the seventeenth century to the Hamilton (later Rowan Hamilton) family in whose possession it still remains.

KILLYLEAGH (WAG 2109)

A panoramic view of the town taken from the lough shore. The lough played a prominent role in the life of the residents for both business, with the harbour, and pleasure, with the yacht club, already active in 1910 with its August regatta.

STRANGFORD LOUGH AT KILLYLEAGH (WAG 2097)
While everything else is changing some things remain the same. It is hoped that the beauty of the Strangford Lough with its innumerable little inlets and natural harbours will never change.

OTHER PHOTOGRAPHS FROM THE W. A. GREEN COLLECTION ON THE ARDS NOT INCLUDED IN THIS SELECTION

Prints of these, and the photographs in the book, may be obtained from the photographic department of the Ulster Folk and Transport Museum, Cultra, Co. Down.

WAG 49	Quintin Castle
WAG 330	Greyabbey
WAG 331	Greyabbey
WAG 331A	Greyabbey
WAG 332	Greyabbey
WAG 334	Greyabbey
WAG 610	Portaferry
WAG 879	Mahee Island
WAG 880	Mahee Island
WAG 882	Mahee Island
WAG 947	Comber Road
WAG 1696	Killyleagh Castle
WAG 1698	Killyleagh Castle
WAG 1700	Barbican, Killyleagh
WAG 1784	Scrabo Tower
WAG 1787	View of Scrabo
WAG 1788	Scrabo across Strangford
WAG 1792A	Old Priory, Newtownards
WAG 1795	Scrabo Hill
WAG 1833	Kircubbin
WAG 1839	Kircubbin harbour
WAG 1853	Quintin Castle
WAG 1856	Carrowdore Castle
WAG 1857	Carrowdore Castle
WAG 1858	Carrowdore Castle
WAG 1868	Ballywalter
WAG 2085	Ballywalter
WAG 2086	Ballywalter
WAG 2092	Mahee Island
WAG 2096	Rainey Island
WAG 2098	Scrabo from Comber
WAG 2100	Mahee from Oldtown
WAG 2101	Mahee & Causeway
WAG 2102	Castle & Causeway
WAG 2104	Scrabo across Comber River
WAG 2105	Scrabo Hill
WAG 2106	Scrabo
WAG 2106A	Mahee island from the tea room
WAG 2213	Comber River
WAG 2495	Scrabo
WAG 2495A	Scrabo
WAG 2495B	Scrabo
WAG 2635	Scrabo from Bradshaws Brae
WAG 2664	Scrabo from east
WAG 2665	Scrabo with harvest
WAG 2729	Cloghy
WAG 2729A	Cloghy
WAG 2736	Portavogie
WAG 2742	Scrabo
WAG 2985	Mahee Island
WAG 2986	Mahee Island
WAG 3037	Greyabbey
WAG 3074	Strangford Lough
WAG 3074A	Strangford Lough
WAG 3239	Portavogie Harbour
WAG 3302	Newtownards
WAG 3313	Portavogie harbour
WAG 3334	Comber River
WAG 3354	Portavogie Harbour
WAG 3364	Portavogie Harbour
WAG 3450	Killyleagh castle
WAG 3452	Quintin Castle
WAG 3521	Objects from Mahee
WAG 3522	Cross on Church gable, Mahee
WAG 3523	Old Church, Mahee
WAG 3526	Round Tower, Mahee
WAG 3528	Sundial, Mahee
WAG 3565	Quarry, Scrabo
WAG 3566	Geological feature, Scrabo
WAG 3614	Burial Urns, Comber
WAG 3633	Quintin Castle

SOURCES

In the research for this book the publications of the Ulster Architectural Historical Society were extremely valuable. The relevant volumes were **East Down** (Belfast, 1973) compiled by C. E. B. Brett; **Portaferry and Strangford** (Belfast, 1973) compiled by G. P. Bell, C. E. B. Brett, and Sir Robert Matthew; **Court houses and Market Houses of the Province of Ulster** (Belfast, 1973) C. E. B. Brett; and Ballywalter Park (Belfast, 1985). Also helpful was **Historic Monuments of Northern Ireland** (sixth edition, Belfast, 1983) Department of the Environment for Northern Ireland.

Other recent, useful publications include: **County Down 100 years ago: a guide and directory** (Dublin, 1886, reprinted Belfast, 1988) G. H. Bassett; **Northern Ireland: a census map** (Dublin, 1978) ed. Paul A. Compton; **An Archaeological Survey of County Down** (Belfast, 1966) Government of Northern Ireland; **Mountstewart** (National Trust of Northern Ireland, 1956) The Marchioness of Londonderry; **Scrabo Golf Club 75th Anniversary Souvenir Brochure** (Newtownards, 1982); **A History of Congregations in the Presbyterian Church in Ireland 1610-1982** (Belfast, 1982) compiled by the Presbyterian Historical Society of Ireland; **Irish Historical Statistics: population 1921-1971** (Dublin, 1978) ed. W. E. Vaughan and A. J. Fitzpatrick; and **Shadows on Glass** (Belfast, 1977) B. M. Walker.

A number of earlier works provided helpful information. They include: Cassell's **Gazetteer of Great Britain and Ireland** (London, 1893); **The Ancient and Present State of the County of Down** (Dublin, 1744) Walter Harris; **In Praise of Ulster** (Belfast, 1938) Richard Hayward; **Millisle and**

Ballycopeland Presbyterian Church: a short history (Newtownards, 1934) Rev. T. Kilpatrick; **A history of the County of Down** (Dublin, 1875) Alexander Knox; **Topographical dictionary of Ireland** (2nd edition, Dublin, 1846) Samuel Lewis; **The Bangor Season** (Bangor, 1885) W. G. Lyttle; **Montgomery Manuscripts: colonisation of the Ards** (Belfast, 1830) William Montgomery; **Historical Account of the Diocese of Down and Connor Ancient and Modern** (Vol. I Dublin, 1878; Vol. II Dublin, 1880) Rev. James O'Laverty; **Official Guide to the County Down and the Mountains of Mourne** (Belfast, 1900) Robert Lloyd Praeger; and **Shaw's Tourist's Picturesque Guide to Carlingford bay and the County Down** (London, 1877).

The following articles also provided useful information: **Inishargy through the ages** (1967) Prof. J. C. Beckett; **Belfast Naturalist Field Club Proceedings** 1918-19, 1927-28; **Irish embroidery and lacemaking** by Elizabeth Boyle in **Ulster Folklife** Vol. 12; and **Public Transport in Newtownards** by D. B. McNeill in **The Ards Historical Journal** Vol. 9 (1985).

ACKNOWLEDGEMENTS

The photographs in this book are reproduced by kind
permission of the trustees of the Ulster Folk and Transport
Museum. My grateful thanks go to Ken Anderson of the
photography department at the museum; also to Ronnie
Adams, Linda Ballard and Michael McCaughan at the museum
for their help. I should also like to thank Brian M. Walker and
Margaret McNulty at Friar's Bush Press for their constructive
criticism. During the course of my research the following
people provided great assistance: the staff of the Newspaper
Library in the Central Library, Belfast; the staff of the Linen
Hall Library; G. Bennett, Northern Ireland Electricity;
James McKeag; Mr McCorriston; Mrs Reid; Mrs Wilson; Mrs
Bailie; Mr Burns; Mrs Crowe; Mr Magill; Mr Graham; Ms C.
Charley; Ms E. Young; Dr W. E. St C. Crosbie; and finally
Robert Lyle for his encouragement.